EXP
Cats

Written by: Kirsty Neale
Illustrated by: Adrian Chesterman

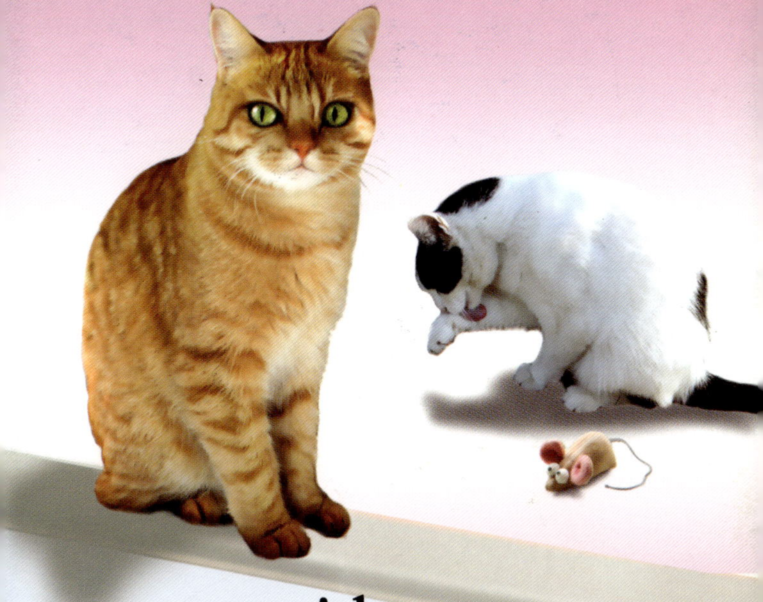

igloo

What is a Cat?

Cats were first kept as pets because they were good at catching the rats and mice that ate people's food. Although most pet, or **domesticated**, cats now live comfortably indoors, they're still natural hunters.

pointed ears

large eyes

long tail helps with balance

long legs

sensitive whiskers

Cats have flexible bodies, sleek fur and rounded heads. Although pets, they move their bodies like **wild cats**, even when they're playing.

smooth fur

paws

Cats have five toes on each front paw,

Claws

A cat's claws slide back inside its paws when they're not being used. This stops them from getting blunt. The claws shoot back out to catch and grip **prey** when the cat is hunting.

toe with relaxed claw

toe with extended claw

◀ A cat uses its claws for climbing, hunting and protecting itself by scratching.

All cats are carnivores, or meat-eaters. When a cat yawns, you can see its teeth, including its four long canines, used for holding prey, such as mice.

but only four toes on each back paw.

5

Sleek Movers

Cats are incredible movers, and excellent judges of size and distance. They can easily climb trees and walk along narrow ledges without losing their balance.

Unlike most animals, when cats walk, they move two legs on one side, then two legs on the other side, putting one foot exactly in front of the other.

Cats use their whiskers to judge whether

Cats can climb down from high places, but they prefer to jump. If they fall, their body twists in mid-air so they nearly always land safely on all four feet.

▼ A cat can sprint at up to 30 miles (48 km) per hour — the same speed that a car is allowed to travel in many towns and cities.

▼ A cat **stalks** its prey by moving very slowly and silently, keeping its body close to the ground. When it gets close enough, it **pounces**.

or not they can fit through small gaps.

7

Big Cats

Domesticated cats belong to the same **family** as **big cats**, which includes lions, tigers and cheetahs. Although they're different in size, they behave in many similar ways.

▲ The cheetah is the fastest land animal. It can chase prey at up to 70 miles (112 km) per hour.

◀ Jaguars live in the jungles of South and Central America. They're often found near water, and have been known to hunt small crocodiles.

From standing still, a cheetah can

Lions live in a small family group, or pride. They hunt together, share the food they catch, and even **groom** each other to remove insects and keep their fur clean.

Tigers are the largest and most powerful of the big cats. They hunt on their own in the jungles of India and **Southeast Asia**.

reach top speed in just 3 seconds!

Long-haired Cats

Unusually for a pet cat, the Turkish Van loves water and is sometimes called 'the swimming cat'.

Long-haired cats were first bred about 100 years ago. They were bred for their soft, silky fur, which needs grooming every day to remove tangles and dirt.

Although adult Birmans are cream

A Birman cat has soft, golden or creamy-brown fur and white feet. It is the sacred cat of Myanmar in Southeast Asia.

Turkish Angora cats have long, silky, often shimmery white fur. They sometimes have one blue eye and one green or amber eye.

Unusual breed

The Red Self Longhair is a rare breed, which used to be known as the Orange. It often has trouble breathing through its very flat nose.

◀ Maine Coon cats can grow very large. They are the oldest long-haired breed in America, and are named after their long, bushy, **raccoon**-like tail.

and brown, the kittens are born white.

Short-haired Cats

Short-haired cats are easier to look after than long-haired cats because they don't need to be groomed every day. All wild cats have short hair.

Burmese cats used to live with monks in Asian temples. They're very friendly cats and don't like being left alone.

With its almond-shaped eyes and large ears, the Abyssinian cat looks like the cats painted thousands of years ago in Ancient Egypt.

The first Sphynx cat was born in

Cornish Rex cats have very short, fine hair. Their coats are wavy and they also have curly whiskers and eyebrows.

Unusual breed

Hairless Sphynx cats have no fur or whiskers. Their skin feels soft and fuzzy, like a peach. They often cuddle up to other animals, or people, to keep warm.

▲ Siamese cats have long, creamy-white bodies, dark pointed faces and bright blue eyes. They're playful and intelligent, and use their loud, wailing **miaow** to get their owner's attention.

Canada in 1966, and was named Prune!

13

Eyes and Fur

Cats have very good eyesight. Their eyes are designed to spot prey, even in the dark. Their fur keeps them warm, and the patterns help them to hide in grass and bushes.

▶ Tabby cats have striped fur. They're named after the stripy silk cloth once made in a place called Al-Attabiya in Iraq.

◀ In bright light, the black **pupil** of a cat's eye narrows to a slit. When it's dark, the pupils open wide to let in as much light as possible.

14

In medieval times, black cats were

▼ Tortoiseshell cats have ginger, black, brown and white coats. They're also known as calico cats, and are usually female.

▼ Some cats, such as the Russian Blue, have fur that is a single shade.

▶ Ginger cats are also known as red tabby or marmalade cats. Most ginger cats are male.

Cats' eyes seem to glow in the dark. This is because a 'mirror' at the back of each eye reflects any nearby light.

believed to be companions of witches.

Understanding Cats

Cats show how they're feeling by moving different parts of their body. They use their eyes, ears, tails and paws, and also make noises, to communicate with people and other animals.

▶ Young cats that live in the same place sometimes touch noses or rub their heads together to show they're friends.

Cats rub up against people they trust to leave their **scent** on them and get attention. They also **purr** when they're happy.

All cats spend lots of time grooming, or cleaning, themselves. Their rough tongue pulls out bits of dirt when they lick their fur.

Cats take lots of **naps** during the day

A cat 'kneads', or pushes up and down with its feet, when it's feeling safe and secure. It does this to furniture or a person's lap.

When cats feel threatened, they arch their back and make their fur stand on end so they look bigger and more frightening.

to store up energy for hunting at night.

Caring for Your Cat

Cats that live indoors need a food and water bowl, a comfortable bed and a way to get in and out of the house. Long-haired cats also need grooming brushes.

▼ Cats sleep for up to 18 hours a day, so they need a soft bed. The bed should be kept in a warm, quiet place.

▶ To save the furniture, a pet cat needs a scratching post for sharpening its claws.

Cats can be trained to use a real

Long-haired cats need to be brushed every day to remove tangles from their fur. Brushing also allows the owner to check if the cat has got **fleas**.

A litter tray or box is a cat's indoor toilet. It is generally kept in the same room as the cat's food bowl, but not too near it. It needs to be cleaned every day.

A special travel basket is used to carry a cat any distance, for example to the vet if the cat is feeling unwell.

Cats need their own water dish and food bowl. They come and go through a cat flap, or kitty door, which opens in and out.

toilet, and even flush it afterwards!

◀ If a kitten feels lost or frightened, it miaows loudly for its mother.

Having Kittens

A cat usually gives birth to a **litter** of 2 to 5 kittens. As soon as they're born, the mother licks the kittens clean. They snuggle close to her to keep warm, and to drink her milk.

▼ Kittens start to explore when they're about 6 weeks old. They can run and jump, and will try to get inside or underneath things.

20   A male cat is called a tom and a

Cats like to play with toys. Many of them contain catnip, a herb which has a scent that cats really love.

▼ A cat prefers to have her kittens in a safe, dark place, such as a cupboard, where she won't be disturbed. Kittens are often born at night.

female cat is called a queen.

Glossary

Big cats
Big cats include lions, tigers, leopards and jaguars – the only cats that are able to roar. Other big cats include cheetahs, snow leopards and cougars, or pumas.

Domesticated
An animal that has been bred to live with humans.

Family
All cats, big and small, share particular features and ways of behaving, so they are said to belong to one family.

Fleas
Tiny insects that feed on the blood of animals and people.

Grooming
To clean or brush an animal's fur. A cat grooms itself or another animal mainly by licking.

Litter
A group of animals born at the same time, to the same mother.

Miaow
The noise that a cat makes when it wants attention.

Nap
A short sleep.

Pounce
To jump or move quickly to grab and catch something.

Prey
An animal that is hunted by another animal for food.

Pupil
The black part in the middle of an eye that lets light into the eye.

Purr
A soft, ongoing rumbling noise made by a contented cat.

Raccoon
A medium-sized animal common in North America. It has black eye-patches and a bushy, black-and-white striped tail.

Scent
A natural smell.

Southeast Asia
All the countries to the east of India, between China and Australia.

Stalk
To follow behind an animal that is being hunted, keeping as close to it as possible, without being seen or heard.

Wild cats
Untamed cats, including medium-sized cats such as the lynx, that live in the wild and avoid contact with people.